In Silence

Lebi P. Nieves Morán

Lebi P. Nieves Morán

© 2018 Lebi P. Nieves Morán
ISBN: 9781725521650
Cover by @nio.ortiz (Instagram)
Edited by: Jasmine Concepción
First edition: 2018

Lebi P. Nieves Morán

To my family and friends.

Preface

This book was born in the depth of my notebook. Was built precisely *In silence*, I wasn't planning on another book, but my thoughts are loud and my feelings are screamers. My only option is writing.

It doesn't matter the time or the place, I have or had? to release my inner thoughts and feelings, and writing helps or helped. Pain, love, and thoughts are united here without any direction particularly, just words. I guess some silence is needed to help us grow.

Blessings, have a lovely day.

Lebi P. Nieves Morán

Introduction

What is the silence? Is actually the absence of sound? Being in silence can go way more meanings than just that. When I'm in silence it means that I'm observing my surroundings and learning, it means that I'm thinking about what I feel, it means creating, it means growing, it means communication, and it means everything.

Lebi P. Nieves Morán

Poems

1.	Me	14
2.	Conversation	15
3.	Point	16
4.	I miss you	17
5.	I already knew	18
6.	Here	20
7.	The ones	21
8.	Life	22
9.	Shall I	23
10.	You say	24
11.	Truth	26

12.	My heart	27
13.	I feel	28
14.	Wrong	29
15.	Paper	30
16.	Insane	31
17.	A piece	32
18.	This	33
19.	It's OK	34
20.	They're calling	35
21.	He shot me	36
22.	I get nervous	37
23.	I see you	38

24.	I don't love you	39
25.	I don't regret	40
26.	Every Day	41
27.	Ever me	42
28.	Silence and scream	43
29.	Sure	44
30.	Light	45
31.	Concerns	46
32.	If I didn't care	47
33.	Two years ago	49
34.	Your eyes	50
35.	What is wrong?	51

36.	Insult	52
37.	Not again	53
38.	Why is hard?	54
39.	The more	55
40.	Name	56
41.	Scream	57
42.	Your words	58
43.	Now	59
44.	In Search	60
45.	Just go	61
46.	Far	62
47.	He	63

48.	Cold	64
49.	Friends	65
50.	Not Blind	66
51.	I was told	67
52.	Identify	68
53.	On day	69
54.	If I'm lucky	70
55.	Flyaway	73
56.	Dear	77
57.	Pain again	78
58.	Sign	80
59.	Enchanted	81

60.	In silence	83
61.	Now, know	85
62.	I don't care	86
63.	Her	87
64.	I'm still here	89
65.	Thankful	90
66.	Demons	91
67.	No hope	92
68.	A simple note	94
69.	Silence	95
70.	Questions	97
71.	Ice cold eyes	98

72.	Something	100
73.	More	101
74.	Confused	102
75.	Words	103
76.	No use	104
77.	Some stories	106
78.	Hey	107
79.	You	108
80.	I miss you	109
81.	Here	110
82.	Over the years	112
83.	Strong	113

84.	Wrong?	115
85.	Heart?	116
86.	Still?	117
87.	The minute you stayed	118
88.	September	121
89.	Three knocks and one shot	123
90.	Charming	126
91.	Feelings	127
92.	Never after	128
93.	Without colors	129
94.	Kind of hope	130

Me

It's strange that for some reason I don't believe in this. You get mad and then, smile. Like nothing had happened. I miss my own time and my spends of time with those I could share it, without being an obligation.

I'm sorry, yes.

But to me.

Conversation

It goes one way.

Always, YOUR WAY.

Have I had to repeat myself?

No.

Your memory is enhanced, with the ideas your mind creates.

I'm sorry. I'm not sure if you're listening.

But, I'm done.

Point

You are not the bad guy. In fact, there's no one to blame. I guess, time gave you the strength to accept, what you knew from the beginning.

Lebi P. Nieves Morán

I miss you

From the time being. I did miss you.

From now, I'm just used to not seeing you here.

I bet that all those corrections about me needing you in or at some point came in handy. Because I took every single one.

At this point.

I don't know for what you were there.

Lebi P. Nieves Morán

I already knew

Every step and every day.

You reminded me of how important was to not expect any savings from you.

That you weren't there to save me, that I could save my own life.

But also, because all of that, I just needed someone to be there.

And save me from my free time... From bugs

From doing shores on my own.

From my conversations in my solitude.

I already knew that I could save myself.

Lebi P. Nieves Morán

I just needed to know if at least you were fit to save me when I couldn't.

Lebi P. Nieves Morán

There

My heart is pounding...

This time, alone.

Lebi P. Nieves Morán

The ones

There's peace in words that reach people and the ones that were meant to be.

Life

Is too short for those that seek victory.

Shall I...

The courses that are in front of me,

Are dark and small.

Shall I seek deep in the middle of those?

Or make another with my words?

Those dreams I have, are made of gold.

But time and energy are very low.

May I choose another way,

Shall I just prove myself?

Lebi P. Nieves Morán

You say

You swear to me:

Your loyalty,

Your arms and

Your love.

But all I can *believe*,

Is what my thoughts scream for you.

May I speak out loud?

May I be excused from all this around?

All this love you claim to have,

Is worth my secrets in the house?

You may think this is love,

But it's just your own thoughts.

Lebi P. Nieves Morán

Your love is fiction,

Your feelings have shown.

Lebi P. Nieves Morán

Truth

Understanding and accepting

are far away from you.

You may understand,

but you don't accept the truth.

Lebi P. Nieves Morán

My heart

Your heart belongs to me, that was what you said.

My heart belongs to *me*...

And I *choose* to share it with you.

I made a mistake.

Lebi P. Nieves Morán

I feel

There's something that I feel,

every time I see you.

This something... isn't love.

Just lust.

Lebi P. Nieves Morán

Wrong

You are special and great.

My heart is close to the bite.

You are what I don't understand.

My heart is crazy, you know why I'm scared.

May I say words that are sweet,

You should know that I'm complete?

May I tell you this is wrong?

Or your heart already knows?

Lebi P. Nieves Morán

Paper

This wise object contains my soul and tears.

What kind of thing is this, which can carry my soul without wind?

Lebi P. Nieves Morán

Insane

My heart is pounding and I'm happy.

My soul is grateful and I'm happy.

My body is tired and I'm happy.

My mind is amazing and I'm happy.

Lebi P. Nieves Morán

A piece

You had my whole and banished me.

You had me... now there's only fragments.

Lebi P. Nieves Morán

This

I feel this and it's cruel.

The pain is real and it makes me numb.

What should I do if this isn't too good?

My love, this truth is not enough for you.

Lebi P. Nieves Morán

It's ok

It's ok, my heart is broken.

It's ok, I'm not afraid.

It's ok, I can make it.

It's ok, I'm back *again*.

Lebi P. Nieves Morán

They're calling

I seek the time,

as a remaining of my space in here.

I seek the heat,

as a well-known pleasure that penetrates me.

I seek the cold,

as a forgiveness of a well-deserved goodbye.

I seek for you,

as a love that needs to die.

He shot me

They were a few bullets that hit some places that wound me in some way.

But you...

You kill me, hitting my heart.

Lebi P. Nieves Morán

I get nervous

Maybe,

is your smile that intrigues me?

Maybe,

is your inner laugh that possesses me?

Maybe,

is that word of silence that can yell at me?

Maybe,

your eyes have me?

Lebi P. Nieves Morán

I see you

The silence is around.

The darkness is increasing.

But, what are you, sweet friend?

That without words you freeze me.

Counting the moments.

The sparks and drills.

You have the story,

I wish to read.

Lebi P. Nieves Morán

I don't love you

I wish the words that were said,

were sweet and full of heart.

My darling, I mean what I said

and blinded me for you.

You didn't ask for my lies.

You said to always be kind.

But the truth and the kindness were gone,

and now I'm here all alone.

Lebi P. Nieves Morán

I don't regret

Your smile and kindness

were a gift you manage to spread.

With the simplicity of some words,

you blind me in love.

There aren't many men like you around, I know.

It's for that same reason,

there won't be any regret in ever meeting you.

Lebi P. Nieves Morán

Every Day

Every story has a moment when

getting back is the wish and

going forward is the only option.

Every day

Lebi P. Nieves Morán

Ever me

If you ever seek me, I'm here.

If you ever miss me, I'm here.

If you ever love me, I'm here.

If this "Ever" and "me" come,

I'm sure that can stay together.

Lebi P. Nieves Morán

Silence and scream

Hear the sound of my scream,

It's begging for you to stop.

It's clear, my eyes are speaking a human nature.

But it's not the language they thought you.

I'm sorry. Silence and scream, they 'are extreme and close. For this to hold, you need to remember how to love.

Darling, love, and screaming are never a good combination.... unless they have the same root.

Lebi P. Nieves Morán

Sure

My eyes are scared.

My mouth is dry.

My heart is overbeating.

My thoughts are gone.

Lebi P. Nieves Morán

Light

It's inside my tears.

They reflect the shining love I fear.

It's close to being tired.

I'm here.

Concerns

Writing this tear, that seems to be made of concrete.

Being this feeling,

that is bound to this nonsense.

What else is worthy of this time with you?

Have you learned what was bothering us?

It seems to me, this is just us, being with each other.

With the idea, without each other's concerns.

Lebi P. Nieves Morán

If I didn't care

The sound,

space,

the solitude,

in this place.

Is inviting,

I'm denying.

What a few are revising.

Who you are?

At whom goal?

If there was some love,

why you hurt me this much?

This is nothing

and yet, is something.

Because of my love for you,

meant loving.

Would you dare?

If I stared?

Would you love

my soul in anguish?

Have some consideration,

Maybe with some care?

But what I'm asking,

Is what you don't care.

Lebi P. Nieves Morán

Two years ago

I met you,

you didn't talk.

You barely smile,

I couldn't talk.

You didn't pretend,

I could not lie.

You looked lovely,

I met my light.

Lebi P. Nieves Morán

Your eyes

The glare you gave to the room, met my eyes.

I wonder if you know, what I was hoping to find.

I wonder if my smile is the same as always.

Your eyes are cold, how can't I love it?

Lebi P. Nieves Morán

What is wrong?

Taking my time to grasp that moment with you.

Spending each day, wondering.

Did I make the right choice?

I am looking around, I don't see you.

Why it feels wrong?

Lebi P. Nieves Morán

Insult

You said things without thinking.

It hurts.

I bet you don't care.

But why it stuck?

You don't suppose to mean something.

Lebi P. Nieves Morán

Not Again

I begged time to reset.

I begged to stop this.

I begged to God that help me.

I begged to myself, *please not again.*

Lebi P. Nieves Morán

Why is it hard?

I sat down in the sofa.

You leave.

I start talking.

You ignore me.

I try to ignore you.

Then you speak.

And every wall starts to fade.

Then you leave.

Lebi P. Nieves Morán

The more

The more I try,

the less I like it.

My heart is supposed to be beating for someone,

and is not you.

I try to convince myself.

But that is just it.

The more I try,

the more I want you here with me.

Lebi P. Nieves Morán

Name

His name follows me.

His words are heavy.

His eyes are bright and cold.

His mouth is a mystery.

I bet time would heal me

or destroy me.

But it's going to take time to beat me.

Lebi P. Nieves Morán

Scream

My thoughts are storming,

my feelings are being incredulous in front of reality.

Why can't you see this?

Are you pretending not to see it?

Or just trying this thing of forgetting?

This wondering is making me crazy.

My hours have more minutes in them.

Lebi P. Nieves Morán

Your words

Your heart is full of words,

kindness flows out of your actions.

The more I get to know you,

the more scared I am of myself.

I'm attracted to that mystery that your bond to.

I'm intrigued by those words you put in poems.

I'm going deep in the heart with this.

I'm just helpless by your world.

Lebi P. Nieves Morán

Now

I wish I had met you before,

but I'm glad I met you now.

It's not in our time that things happen.

It's always with a good purpose that happens, now.

Lebi P. Nieves Morán

In search

In search of nothing,

I found your sneaky smile.

In search of silence,

I found your voice.

In search of ignorance,

I found brilliance.

In search of you,

I found solitude.

Lebi P. Nieves Morán

Just go

I send my regards to the welcome.

I forget the goodbye on my cheek.

I wish the sound of your voice would vanish.

But, you are gone from here.

These memories are haunting me.

They reach into my mind.

What have I done to your presence?

That is willing to eat me alive.

Lebi P. Nieves Morán

Far

I was thinking about the water.

Watching the sunset end the light.

Thinking this could be my answer.

Failing to accept the lie.

Lebi P. Nieves Morán

He

He came without notice.

I was too busy crying.

I was trying to find calm.

All of a sudden, his arms were around me.

And that's how all began.

He didn't say a word.

He just holds me.

And till this day, he hasn't let me go.

Lebi P. Nieves Morán

Cold

You scream at her.

Like I scream to the toys.

You just insulted her.

Like I did when my brother spoke.

You just said nothing.

When times were warm.

It was never warm.

It was just cold, always.

Lebi P. Nieves Morán

Friends

Distance and memories.

Laughs and karaoke.

This where the amplifications,

of a great time.

But distance is cruel.

It spread you, guys.

But our hearts are connected,

It's better than Wi-Fi.

Lebi P. Nieves Morán

Not blind

I seek this love,

not blind or rough.

This thing that I must understand,

is growing with pain and it hurts.

Lebi P. Nieves Morán

I was told

Not to love, is bad for me.

They say while I breathe.

It's only bad when you're a women.

Man can do as they please.

Please don't say what you think.

Mean don't like it when you speak.

If my mind is full of dreams,

please keep it to yourself, it reeks.

Lebi P. Nieves Morán

Identity

May I say my name?

And words are not yet exonerated.

You may have devalued my childhood,

But my future has no arguing.

In keeping the heart as priceless,

and looking for my happiness.

Might not be in this world,

but I'm sure is more valuable than gold.

Lebi P. Nieves Morán

On day

If you look into my eyes and ask me, why?

Would I be willing to answer or just smile with caution?

I didn't gave up on dreams.

But I was far from your reach.

See me as I did.

Somebody that leaves when you need.

If I'm lucky

If I'm lucky,

I would look into your brown eyes.

And search for the reason to stop looking at the sky.

if I'm lucky,

I could vanish the wisdom in the sentence and go straight to your senses.

If I'm lucky,

I could see the bright shine of that curve

and stay there while you go.

If I'm lucky,

I could admit that I like you,

And get over you.

Lebi P. Nieves Morán

If I'm lucky,

I hope you never find *this* cheesy,

And walk away without traces.

If I'm lucky,

I could stop seeing you doing what you love and feel blessed for just being there.

If I'm lucky,

You would find someone, and I would be there cheering out loud.

If I'm lucky,

One day I would have the courage to tell you the truth and feel happy that you're happy.

If I'm lucky,

I would be all right and my love for you would be just a rough memory.

If I'm lucky,

this silenced pain would die and hopefully my chances of being by your side.

Lebi P. Nieves Morán

Flyaway

Flyaway from the dream of the in conclusion.

Fly far from my sight, a wish I can't find,

that thing call forgets and illusion.

I'm not part of the story you hide,

I'm not that one you deserve.

But, how would or do you know?

How would or do you end up knowing?

If there something is written in my forehead?

Or did you knew right from the start?

Lebi P. Nieves Morán

Flyway my sweet dream

every life has a pike,

And on this day I found the seed

of the one that is causing all this disease.

You are far away from me

and this love is growing without control

if I dare to say, I never like my soul,

it has a mind of her own.

It reaches to each corner of the surroundings

digging in the details and creating damage.

You, my darling, are a damage to a creation,

that thing called division on the senses and collision

on the present.

My dear, I would not let you know the truth,

because there is no sense of the reason,

and no way in the feeling.

It's just a feeling with actions

 that increase my caution.

That thing is killing my options

and still, you smile in within.

I wash that instant and keep myself going,

Lebi P. Nieves Morán

It's no use in forgetting.

It's no use in loving,

it's no use in you leaving.

I might love you less if I did know you

but time is not our friend

I watch you fly away

and my heart pounds harder

Because deep down knows that is not going to change this thing,

whatever it is.

Lebi P. Nieves Morán

Dear

My dear,

my love,

my darling,

      I love you.

Lebi P. Nieves Morán

Pain again

A lovely name that vanishes,

your smile is my panic.

I don't regret this loving

and still, on all these years I'm hoping.

That those memories still on your head,

I don't think I can speak of them.

Because my heart was on pain,

without you knowing my game.

I don't reach in that cave my feels,

I don't speak of those tears.

Lebi P. Nieves Morán

Some memories are better left alone,

and on this day, I hope they did well.

You vanished in this suffering,

without thinking about our bond.

But time has a gift for those who wait,

and pain is not the one playing again.

Sign

Swear to you,

that these memories are done with you.

You choose to stay without being there,

and refuse to love with gloves in your hands.

I wish God gave me a sign.

Well it did,

that's why you're not in my life.

Lebi P. Nieves Morán

Enchanted

I heard stories of the kingdom.

I heard that you where there.

Well, sweetie, I'm not a hero,

but I could be your friend.

I didn't come alone in this forest,

I swim as far from my land,

just to see you smiling,

at least for the moment, I had.

I don't see my life consumed,

on dungeons or cliffs.

Lebi P. Nieves Morán

I just see you giving me your hand,

and both leaving without a scratch.

Lebi P. Nieves Morán

In silence

In silence, I wait.

I don't know who you are?

But I'm awake.

If you see me standing there,

I'm watching you being yourself.

I don't want to let you know my feelings,

because there's too much I fear.

My darling,

I see you there.

I don't know how I could be there with you.

My pain is silence for your existence,

Lebi P. Nieves Morán

I'm crying my pain.

In silence for you,

because I can be there with you,

but I refuse.

Lebi P. Nieves Morán

Now, know

I don't know how much love there's in my head?

I don't care if you left or what day you stayed.

What would now be of me?

What do you know?

Why don't you know?

Lebi P. Nieves Morán

I don't care

If in this day

I see you being yourself,

I see myself being there.

Just telling you why

I don't care.

Life comes here,

to see me being there for you.

Why I don't care?

Why I don't?

Why I don't care anymore?

Lebi P. Nieves Morán

Her

She said: "I could not

make you believe that I was wrong"

I don't blame her,

it was easy to convince me.

She did everything she could to make me less than

her, but it was my fault to never see this.

She was mean to the core and still,

her eyes would have that deep darkness that her

bright smile could not surpass.

Lebi P. Nieves Morán

She was and she is gone.

Gone for my sake,

Gone for good,

Gone with the time,

until she die.

Lebi P. Nieves Morán

I'm still here

"Push her down to cave",

that was your thought.

Bury my talents was your goal,

I'm here.

I'm still here.

Lebi P. Nieves Morán

Thankful

I see the sky every day,

feeling happy that I got to see it.

Each day is a new creation,

and I have a free pass to admire it.

Lebi P. Nieves Morán

Demons

They shake my bed for fear,

they come and knock at my door in despair.

They scream at my ear for attention,

 they scratch my windows for thoughts.

But that day,

their breathing where near my feet.

Lebi P. Nieves Morán

No hope

"I can't",

I said to myself.

When all seems wrong.

I repeat,

"I can't",

but this time, was for others.

I saw the pain in their eyes.

I heard the pain in my voice.

I repeated the words that damaged me.

To those that needed words of hope.

Lebi P. Nieves Morán

I guess that is just what I believed,

that happen that day.

A simple note

You become that same thing you judge,

if you don't keep analyzing your actions.

The *whys* on your life are important,

and more when you want to grow.

Lebi P. Nieves Morán

Silence

They were never a better action,

They were never a better sound.

If one word was in motion,

was the one that begins with the letter *I*?

The loneliness of the surroundings,

the screams of my mind.

Was I always so busy?

Dealing with matters of the life?

Lebi P. Nieves Morán

I didn't wanted to leave you,

you left me here in the dark.

But in some obscure places,

the tiniest light looks more bright.

In silence I forget,

cry and reset.

In silence, I stay,

looking forward to today.

Lebi P. Nieves Morán

Questions

I argue with knowledge,

this silence of goodbyes.

I struggle in pieces,

with my friendliest smile.

But.

what can I do with this feeling towards you?

What can I do if I dare to accept you?

Ice cold eyes

They follow me without a whisper.

They hunt and prey my soul.

Is there madness inside you?

Or just ghost of wrong?

From this place,

The sadness,

emptiness,

and solitude is a happy place.

These things resembled your soul.

Lebi P. Nieves Morán

Deep inside my heart,

I just volunteered to adventure this path.

But you?

Would you let me pass?

Something

There's something always more than the word itself.

Lebi P. Nieves Morán

More

I have been told to love,

I have been told to live.

But darling, what am I doing here?

With this tears and more fear?

Confused

There are words that are around.

They're being held in the ground.

My heart doesn't seem to fight.

My mind lacks light.

If you knew my care for YOU.

If you knew I want to be THERE.

Seem my wishes are numb.

Seems my wishes are just hurt.

Lebi P. Nieves Morán

Words

They come and go.

They say and run.

They hide and show.

They're your words.

No use

I manage to escape those that mention you,

keeping silence.

When I want to tell how well I know you.

Still.

I'm quiet.

My own actions destroy the commitment I made to forget about you.

But your responses, your absences, your turn away looks... They all vanish.

Lebi P. Nieves Morán

There's no use, inside this heart.

The reason is not part of this nature.

You, you and you.

Make each part of this nonsense, my truth.

You changed with me.

Why?

There's no use.

I need to say goodbye.

Lebi P. Nieves Morán

Some stories

I hear them.

They're all there.

Simple and complicated.

Soft and cranky.

Some words.

Some ends.

Some, something...

That someday would end.

Lebi P. Nieves Morán

Hey

I saw you yesterday.

You didn't looked at me.

It seems like a sin is made if you did.

It's a shame.

I like you.

But the reality is bitter.

Moving on.

Lebi P. Nieves Morán

You

I'm dead inside.

I feel like you just vanished my soul.

I'm scared for my life.

I feel that our love was killed by you.

Lebi P. Nieves Morán

I miss you

From the time being. I did miss you.

From now. I'm just used to not seeing you here.

I bet that all those corrections about me needing you in some point came in handy.

Because I took every single one of them.

At this point.

I don't know for what you were.

Lebi P. Nieves Morán

Here

I wish you were here.

It's simply the desire,

The reality is difficult.

You are gone

And I miss you.

What can I do?

To stop this feeling?

It has grown over the years.

Why now?

Lebi P. Nieves Morán

Why not sooner?

You had to go for me to miss you?

Why everything has to happen this way?

Missing when is too late to solve something.

I had no idea I loved you then.

Imagine my surprise!

Lebi P. Nieves Morán

Over the years

Over the years I had to wonder …

Did I ever show you the love I find now?

If I'm teaching good values?

If I'm doing things right with your daughter?

I wonder…

If everything is going to be all right?

If inside of me, still something from you?

Lebi P. Nieves Morán

Strong

Being strong is lonely.

Being small is exhausting.

Being woman is crazy.

Being without you is painful.

Thanks for everything.

Believe it or not, I still suffer your depart.

Seeing her like this is not easy.

I wish I can put some of my strength in her heart,

And take some of her pain out of her.

But who am I to tell her what to do?

I'm just a small teacup that comes and goes,

That suffers in silence and gives the lecture when is needed.

I miss you. She misses you.

I need you. She needs you.

I love you. She can't live without you.

Lebi P. Nieves Morán

Wrong?

For the moment everything has stopped. Those words hit me like a bullet. I knew it deep down… But why they came to my heart so sharp? So cruel? Then again I knew and that was that. I shoot them well directed, hurting my heart but not my soul. Because sometimes we have to make mistakes to do then, the right thing and this was the right thing… I knew it and deep down so did you. This was our goodbye and great mistake of love. Not because the love never was between us, it's because we leave the reason far away. For your happiness and a farewell; for me a goodbye and a shoot in my heart.

Heart?

I guess this was it. I went to the place that I had with you and started to remember you. It was hard. The air was colder. My eyes where cloudy. I hate that feeling! The feeling that you are about to burst into tears, but retain them. Because is not the moment to realize the truth about the things. Is the moment to ignore the pieces of your heart and become an individual without a heart. I know for once that my words have got you, because you never called. You just stop fighting for us. You gave up as I did. But with the only difference that I fought for us, a little. You instead leave it there. Without a fight, without words, without an action… Weak-hearted.

Lebi P. Nieves Morán

Still?

Still hurts the living memory in the back of my head. I believe that the pain is looking for a house to stay in.

I guess that the heart wasn't enough.

But still, you are here. Waiting to attack. When my life keeps running. You are not what I have expected because I really have loved you. Still, it drains me that my memory is better in giving me ideas that would never come out of my mouth. You are that ghost that I didn't want to lose. That certain things that you know that it kills but then again doesn't leave. Is like you were so attached to it beyond words. Is like I want to have you… but like you have pictured yourself. Not that person that you are. So I rather look for better.

Lebi P. Nieves Morán

The minute that you stayed

After long hours of great thinking, I started to think about you. I believe that is the brain that has to stop thinking about an important thing and decided that is time to change the subject. Well is time to dedicate a minute to talk about you or in other words to think whatever it is that I should think about you. You are not the insane bastard that I became to love. Just that somebody that came into my life and rebuild me in the most bastard way. So, of course, I have to admit something bad about you. Is time I stop saying how great it was staying in silence and letting all go the way you wanted to go? My words mean something in some way and that is why I'm just saying what I know. Oh! I know what you may think? Why think about this now when the time has gone away so fast? Why say things that may hurt the spirit that is hearing what I haven't talk? Well simple… I got tired. I loved you. You just didn't.

Is not that last part that actually beat the hell out of me. Is the fact that I had to admit to myself and actually telling you what you can't face. I hate that from me. Me and my self-conscious. "Better to love that wasn't love," some idiots said. Well yeah, happiness is a big issue for me. So thanks for being the idiot that change my great expectations. You didn't show me heaven. The love that I had for you showed me that. You were just a nothing that shows me greatness and for that I always be thankful. But believe me, loving you was easy. I hope you are better and safe. I don't hate you, I have no regrets. I just don't know a better way to stop this stupid feeling.

I don't wish I haven't meted you, in fact, I'm glad. I just hope that in some weird way you can be happy and see what I saw in us. That thing that you weren't part of it. I wish you well. I would try to keep my way. But forgive me for this. Because I don't know how you got over this.

Lebi P. Nieves Morán

September

This day I'm happy

You were born this day.

I can't see you this day,

I won't do it your way.

It has been five months,

Since I had seen your face.

But what can I do?

Your birthday is today.

I can't see your eyes,

I have loved you too much.

Lebi P. Nieves Morán

I can't see your smile,

It would kill me like a shot.

May I just pretend you exist.

Far away, not close to me.

May I just make it through this day

Loving you as always, including today.

Lebi P. Nieves Morán

Three knocks and one shot

I was driving in one direction. The light was brighter than the usual. I knew where I was going but I couldn't name the place where I was heading. Finally, I stop the car in front of a house with multiples windows. It was a one piece house. It didn't have a second floor or neighbors close to it.

I went inside and looked for my grandmother who had a room in the house. I didn't stop to talk to anybody. I entered the house and looked at her, when I got to the room. She was smiling and staring at me. *Like she was waiting for me.* I sat down and start a conversation with her. We laugh and stare at each other with a lot to say, but something was wrong. Words didn't come out of her. The silence was being a winner in this visit. So

I continue to touch her hair and smile at her. My heart was sad; I knew that I had to go in some time. That this time won't come back for a while.

Then, I looked at my watch, which I didn't remember that I had on. I tell her that I have to go. She looks at me with understanding and gives me a kiss as an incline myself for her to reach my cheeks. I look at her one last time and continue walking away from her. With only her smile in my head. Once I reach outside her room I saw a man with no hair. I still can't remember his face. I ask him if he can go to my grandmother and be there with her for a while, just to talk to her and give her some company. He nods.

I went to my car and start the engine. I drove away but things started to get blur once I head to the street. Then, the blur wasn't just the problem, I began to hear a knock in a door. I looked around but nothing. Now everything went dark and I woke up.

Another knock, I opened my eyes widely. I realized that I was sleeping. I looked around. I was in my bed and the light in my room were as always. The third knock follows. I gave up on ignoring the knocks, I got out of my bed and open the door. It was my mother and brother with sleepy but sad faces.

-What's wrong? I asked.

-"Grandma died" My mother reply.

That's the only thing I heard. I close the door, back to my bed. Got the sheets around my body and pretend that this was the real dream.

Lebi P. Nieves Morán

Charming

I was avoiding your existence

Pretending to live.

And with some persistence,

I manage to be.

In some sense

In love

In some matter lost.

Lebi P. Nieves Morán

Feelings

The secret was reveal with your absence.

Near my thoughts were your words.

But.

No love is worth tears when there's no heart.

I see them running figuring life in the way.

I see them standing there, enjoying the sun and taking shelter for the rain.

I see them... why can't they see me?

Never after

I stand

You leave

I stay

You be

Without me

a never

ever

After.

That you

Don't

seek.

Lebi P. Nieves Morán

Without colors

Is waiting the darkness,

dead silence is hunting.

Life is clouded,

and light is brightest.

I choose to forget the ticking,

expect the even madness.

See what without colors,

can be reach.

Lebi P. Nieves Morán

Kind of hope

Please run

I'm no good

For any one

I see my reflection

It's not me who I look

Is someone else

The rage that runs within veins

I gain control of nonsense

I stray my words with love

Deep in my core I'm rotten

Lebi P. Nieves Morán

Without having any kind of hope

Lebi P. Nieves Morán

Thanks for reading.

To my friends and family, thanks for the patience and the love. I hope time keeps making me more attentive of your kindness. Blessings for all and more than grateful of your existence.

You can write me:

Lebip.nievesmoran@gmail.com

Lebi P. Nieves Morán

Other book:

Made in the USA
Middletown, DE
09 March 2022